495

GENESIS

WALKING WITH GOD

25 Studies for Individuals or Groups

MARGARET FROMER &
SHARREL KEYES

Harold Shaw Publishers • Wheaton, Illinois

ISBN 0-87788-297-5

Cover photo © 1994 by Luci Shaw

99 98 97

12 11 10 9 8 7 6 5 4

CONTENTS

HOW TO USE THIS STUDYGUIDE

Fisherman studyguides are based on the inductive approach to Bible study. Inductive study is discovery study; we discover what the Bible says as we ask questions about its content and search for answers. This is quite different from the process in which a teacher *tells* a group *about* the Bible and what it means and what to do about it. In inductive study God speaks directly to each of us through his Word.

A group functions best when a leader keeps the discussion on target, but this leader is neither the teacher nor the "answer person." A leader's responsibility is to *ask*—not *tell*. The answers come from the text itself as group members examine, discuss, and think together about the passage.

There are four kinds of questions in each study. The first is an *approach question*. Used before the Bible passage is read, this question breaks the ice and helps you focus on the topic of the Bible study. It begins to reveal where thoughts and feelings need to be transformed by Scripture.

Some of the earlier questions in each study are *observation questions* designed to help you find out basic facts—who, what, where, when, and how.

When you know what the Bible says you need to ask, *What does it mean?* These *interpretation questions* help you to discover the writer's basic message.

Application questions ask, *What does it mean to me?* They challenge you to live out the Scripture's life-transforming message.

Fisherman studyguides provide spaces between questions for jotting down responses and related questions you would like to raise in the group. Each group member should have a copy of the studyguide and may take a turn in leading the group.

A group should use any accurate, modern translation of the Bible such as the *New International Version,* the *New American Standard Bible,* the *Revised Standard Version,* the *New Jerusalem Bible,* or the *Good News Bible.* (Other translations or paraphrases of the Bible may be referred to when additional help is needed.) Bible commentaries should not be brought to a Bible study because they tend to dampen discussion and keep people from thinking for themselves.

SUGGESTIONS FOR GROUP LEADERS

1. Read and study the Bible passage thoroughly beforehand, grasping its themes and applying its teachings for yourself. Pray that the Holy Spirit will "guide you into truth" so that your leadership will guide others.

2. If the studyguide's questions ever seem ambiguous or unnatural to you, rephrase them, feeling free to add others that seem necessary to bring out the meaning of a verse.

3. Begin (and end) the study promptly. Start by asking someone to pray for God's help. Remember, the Holy Spirit is the teacher, not you!

4. Ask for volunteers to read the passages out loud.

5. As you ask the studyguide's questions in sequence, encourage everyone to participate in the discussion. If some are silent, ask, "What do you think, Heather?" or, "Dan, what can you add to that answer?" or suggest, "Let's have an answer from someone who hasn't spoken up yet."

6. If a question comes up that you can't answer, don't be afraid to admit that you're baffled! Assign the topic as a research project for someone to report on next week.

7. Keep the discussion moving and focused. Though tangents will inevitably be introduced, you can bring the discussion back to the topic at hand. Learn to pace the discussion so that you finish a study each session you meet.

8. Don't be afraid of silences: some questions take time to answer and some people need time to gather courage to speak. If silence persists, rephrase your question, but resist the temptation to answer it yourself.

9. If someone comes up with an answer that is clearly illogical or unbiblical, ask him or her for further clarification: "What verse suggests that to you?"

10. Discourage Bible-hopping and overuse of cross-references. Learn all you can from *this* passage, along with a few important references suggested in the studyguide.

11. Some questions are marked with a ♦. This indicates that further information is available in the Leader's Notes at the back of the guide.

12. For further information on getting a new Bible study group started and keeping it functioning effectively, read Gladys Hunt's *You Can Start a Bible Study Group* and *Pilgrims in Progress: Growing through Groups* by Jim and Carol Plueddemann.

SUGGESTIONS FOR GROUP MEMBERS

1. Learn and apply the following ground rules for effective Bible study. (If new members join the group later, review these guidelines with the whole group.)

2. Remember that your goal is to learn all that you can *from the Bible passage being studied.* Let it speak for itself without using Bible commentaries or other Bible passages. There is more than enough in each assigned passage to keep your group productively occupied for one session. Sticking to the passage saves the group from insecurity and confusion.

3. Avoid the temptation to bring up those fascinating tangents that don't really grow out of the passage you are discussing. If the topic is of common interest, you can bring it up later in informal conversation following the study. Meanwhile, help each other stick to the subject!

4. Encourage each other to participate. People remember best what they discover and verbalize for themselves. Some people are naturally shyer than others, or they may be afraid of making a mistake. If your discussion is free and friendly and you show real interest in what other group members think and feel, they will be more likely to speak up. Remember, the more people involved in a discussion, the richer it will be.

5. Guard yourself from answering too many questions or talking too much. Give others a chance to express themselves. If you are one who participates easily, discipline yourself by counting to ten before you open your mouth!

6. Make personal, honest applications and commit yourself to letting God's Word change you.

PART ONE

BEGINNINGS

Who are we? Who made us? Why are we here? These are some of the big questions answered in this book. Its name, *Genesis,* means "beginning." We'll see the beginning of the original relationship between God and his creation and the breakdown of that relationship caused by sin. Because of humankind's continued rebellion, God sends a great flood upon the earth. There is a new beginning after the flood, but the sinlessness of Eden is never regained, and the drama of God's plan of redemption continues.

WHAT DOES IT MEAN TO LIVE IN GOD'S WORLD?

Genesis 1:1–2:3

1. What is the most creative project you have attempted?

♦ **Read Genesis 1:1–2:3.**

2. What words or phrases are repeated in this passage?
What are the effects of this repetition?

3. Which words get the most emphasis? Why?

4. What do we know about human beings from this chapter
(1:26-30)?

---

5. What do we learn about God from this entire passage?

♦ **6.** Considering what we have just discovered about God, what does it mean for us to be created in God's image (1:26-27)?

7. How do you express the fact that you are made in God's image?

In what ways do you fail to express God's image?

8. How might you change in order to be more contented with yourself and more pleasing to God?

9. Pray, praising God for one thing you have learned about him from this study.

HOW DOES GOD MEET OUR NEEDS?

Genesis 2:4-25

1. What is the most pleasant aspect of your work? The most difficult?

Read Genesis 2:4-25.

2. What reasons did Adam and Eve have to be thankful to God? Note the verse from which you discover each reason as well as what you have discovered.

3. What differences do you see between the way God gave life to the creatures of the water, air, and earth and the way God gave life to Adam and Eve? (Compare Genesis 1:20-21, 24-25 with 1:27 and 2:7.)

4. There would be both pleasures and responsibilities for Adam as he kept God's command to work the ground and take care of it. What do you think the pleasures would be? What would be the responsibilities?

♦ **5.** In what ways would Adam and Eve benefit by obeying God's command not to eat the fruit of the tree of the knowledge of good and evil?

6. What would you enjoy about naming the animals? Why would it require some work on your part?

7. How would these jobs (working the ground, obeying God, naming the animals) prepare Adam and Eve to fulfill God's command to subdue the earth and rule over it (1:28-29)?

8. Why do you think God said it wasn't good for man to be alone?

♦ **9.** Why did God show Adam the animals first as he looked for a mate?

10. In what ways was the woman more suitable for Adam?

11. How does this chapter add to what we have already learned about the character of God from Genesis 1?

12. From our discussion of God's provisions for Adam and Eve, what conclusions can we draw about what people need?

13. What has God given to you that shows he knows your needs?

WHY IS DISOBEYING GOD SO SERIOUS?

Genesis 3

1. What is the best excuse you've heard for disobedience?

Read Genesis 3.

♦ **2.** Retell the story, setting the major events in order. (Try this with your Bible closed.)

3. What was the difference between Eve's answer to the serpent in verse 3 and God's original command in 2:17?

What does her addition suggest about her attitude toward God's command? (What might she have been thinking about the tree before the serpent came on the scene?)

4. How do you make God's commands more restrictive than he makes them?

5. Why might it seem easier for Eve to believe the serpent than to believe God?

6. What rationalizations do you use when you are about to disobey God?

7. How did Adam and Eve respond to God when they were caught? Why?

8. How were their attitudes toward themselves, toward each other, and toward God affected by their disobedience?

What would life have been like if they had completely obeyed God?

9. How would you defend the justice of God's sentence on the serpent and Adam and Eve?

10. In verses 21-24 how did God provide for their new needs? Why was being sent from the Garden a provision and not a punishment?

11. What have you learned from our discussion today that will most help you to resist your next temptation to sin?

WHAT IS MY RESPONSE TO SIN?

Genesis 4

1. What kind of gift do you most like to receive?

♦ **Read Genesis 4.**

2. This is the first mention of offerings. Why would anyone bring offerings to God?

♦ **3.** Assume for the moment that God would be equally pleased with either an offering of a lamb or of fruit. What reasons are suggested in the text for why God accepted Abel's offering and not Cain's (verses 3-5)?

4. Restate God's warning to Cain in your own words (verses 6-7).

What kind of person was God trying to help Cain become?

5. Compare Genesis 3:9-11 with Genesis 4:9. Why do you suppose God confronted Cain with his sin by asking questions?

What was God really asking? What response would he have liked?

♦ **6.** In what ways was Cain's punishment a severe one? In what ways did his punishment fit the crime?

7. What do verses 13-22 show of God's continuing provision for Cain?

8. What word would you choose to describe Lamech's attitude toward sin (verses 19-24)?

9. What differences do you see between Adam and Eve's response to sin, Cain's response to his sin, and Lamech's response to sin?

10. What do you know about the nature of sin from this chapter?

11. How does God warn you about sin in your own life?

12. In your own battle with sin, what difference does it make that you can call on the name of the Lord (verse 26)?

We will not study the lineage from Adam to Noah recorded in Genesis 5, but read this chapter on your own for continuity, noting God's relationship with humanity over generations.

WHAT IS IT LIKE TO WALK WITH GOD IN A SINFUL WORLD?

Genesis 6:5–7:24

1. What is the greatest hindrance you face in walking with God?

Read Genesis 6:5–7:24.

♦ **2.** In 6:5-13, what did God see when he looked at the earth?

Compare how God felt now with how he felt initially after creation.

♦ **3.** In these verses, what words and phrases describe Noah?

4. What evidence do you find of God's affection for and approval of Noah?

5. What words and phrases so far show how strongly God feels about sin?

6. In order to walk with someone (rather than have them walk with you), what do you have to do?

7. Pretend you're Noah. In what ways would it have been hard to walk with God in the kind of world pictured in chapter 6?

In what ways would it have been helpful to walk with God in that world?

8. What words and phrases in chapter 7 add to our picture of what Noah did to "walk with God"?

9. What would you have found especially hard about living on the ark?

10. In light of Noah's example, what can you do to walk with God? Be specific.

HOW DOES MY WALK WITH GOD AFFECT OTHERS?

Genesis 8 – 9

1. Who has been most influential in your life, for good or for bad?

Read Genesis 8.

2. What was Noah waiting for before he could get off the ark?

3. Can you think of a time when you were tired of being cooped up and didn't understand why God was so slow to act? What do you do when you get impatient with God?

4. If you were Noah, what might you have prayed at the altar?

5. Why do you think God is pleased by our worship?

Read Genesis 9:1-17.

6. In God's covenant with Noah, what were the responsibilities God gives to people?

7. In what ways was God again providing for his creatures' needs?

8. Glance back through chapters 6–9. Who benefited by Noah's walk with God?

♦ **9.** In what ways do other people benefit because you walk with God?

Read Genesis 9:18-29.

10. What is your impression of Noah from this passage?
Of his sons?

♦ **11.** Why do you think this story is included in Genesis?

12. Using the insight you have gained from studying
Genesis 1–9, what would you say to someone who tries to
justify his or her actions by saying, "I'm just one person,
what I do doesn't matter"?

*Read Genesis 10 and 11 on your own before the next
study. About this time in history, many of the great ancient
cities of the world were being built. Babel, with its great
gates, double walls, intricate decorations and hanging gar-
dens was, by the time of Nebuchadnezzar (600 B.C.), one of
the seven wonders of the ancient world.*

   *This account shows the first time people combined their
efforts toward a common objective. People working together have much greater power than the individual, but
their pride and refusal to depend on God resulted in judgment that brought about the very thing they had tried to
prevent: "The LORD scattered them over the face of the
whole earth" (11:9). God's discipline illustrates graphi-
cally where people should look for real security.*

PART TWO

ABRAHAM

God's redemptive drama in history continues to unfold with the history of Abraham. One of the great patriarchs of faith, Abraham was an imperfect man who exhibited a steadfast faith in his great and powerful God.

We don't know much about Abraham's early life. His father, Terah, was a descendant of Shem, Noah's son, and Abram (as he was called then) lived with his father, brothers, and wife Sarai in Ur of the Chaldeans. At some point Terah set out to move his family to Canaan, but they ended up settling in the city of Haran.

It was in Haran that Abram first heard God's call and promise, and history would never be the same.

WHAT IS THE RESPONSE OF FAITH?

Genesis 12–13

1. What was your first experience of leaving home? How did it affect you?

Read Genesis 12:1-9.

2. What would Abram have had to give up in leaving his country, his people, and his father's household?

3. How did God help Abram obey him?

4. What is significant about Abram's response to God's call?

5. Why did God have to tell Abram when he reached the land promised to his offspring? What was Abram's response this time?

♦ **Read Genesis 12:10-20.**

6. Why did Abram go to Egypt?

7. Why do you think Sarai went along with Abram's plan?

How did God help Sarai in this situation?

8. What did Abram learn about God in Egypt?

Read Genesis 13.

9. Where did Abram go when he left Egypt?

10. Why did Abram suggest that he and Lot separate?

11. What did God then add to what he had already promised Abram (verses 14-17)?

Can you think of any reasons for God's speaking to Abram just then?

12. From these two chapters, how do you see Abram showing his trust in God, both for the immediate present and for the future?

13. How does being obedient in little things help you learn the details of God's promises (plans) for you?

Read Genesis 14 on your own. It describes Abram's rescue of his nephew Lot and the king of Sodom from captivity. The king of Sodom offers Abram a reward, but Abram refuses since he has promised God not to take anything from Sodom, lest the king say that he, and not God, had made Abram rich. This refusal to claim riches rightfully his, in order to protect God's name, is the background against which the events in chapter 15 are set.

WHAT IS INVOLVED IN BELIEVING GOD?

Genesis 15–16

1. When have you experienced a discouraging or frustrating delay of plans?

Read Genesis 15.

2. What was Abram's response to the Lord's promise of a great reward?

3. How did the Lord reassure him?

Why do you think Abram was able to believe what the Lord told him?

4. Why is God pleased by our belief?

♦ **5.** In verse 8 Abram asked, "How can I know?" In what ways did God answer his question?

Why did God take the trouble to tell Abram all the facts in verses 13-16?

6. What did Abram learn about God's character from his answer?

Read Genesis 16.

◆ **7.** What motivated Abram's action in verses 2-4?

8. What were the consequences of their actions for Abram, Sarai, and Hagar?

9. Contrast the Abram you see here with the Abram you saw in Genesis 15.

10. How do you react to long-range promises? Why?

11. What are some danger signals that would help you know you are trying to fulfill God's promises in your own way and your own time?

WHAT DOES IT MEAN TO BE IN A COVENANT RELATIONSHIP WITH GOD?

Genesis 17

1. Think about one of your best friends. What makes your relationship so strong?

♦ **Read Genesis 17.**

2. When God appeared, what did he reveal about himself to Abram? If you were in Abram's shoes, what would it mean to have a God with this name as your God?

♦ **3.** What else did Abram learn about God because of what God promised him (verses 5-8)?

4. What did God ask of Abraham (verses 9-14)?

5. What was Abraham's prayer for Ishmael (verse 18)?

6. In what ways did God honor his request, and in what ways did he refuse it?

7. List all the verses in the chapter in which the term *covenant* appears.

♦ **8.** By using *all* the examples in this chapter, what can we understand about the nature of a covenant? (Is a covenant a promise? A legal statement? A relationship? A sign?)

9. Why is it helpful to have a covenantal sign?

10. What helps *you* remember that you belong to God?

How do other people know you belong to God?

HOW DO I RESPOND TO GOD'S RIGHTEOUS JUDGMENT?

Genesis 18:16–19:38

1. How did your parents punish you when you were a child?

Read Genesis 18:16-33.

2. What reasons did the Lord have for telling Abraham his intentions?

What was Abraham to teach his descendants (verse 19)?

3. What evidence did Abraham have that God was personally interested in both righteousness and justice?

How do you know Abraham took God's judgment seriously?

Read Genesis 19:1-29.

4. What did the two angels find when they got to Sodom?

5. What did Lot's choosing Sodom and staying there say about his priorities?

6. What evidence do we see that Lot's family did not take God's judgment seriously?

7. What reasons does this passage give for God's willingness to save Lot?

8. What modern-day problems do you see in this ancient story of Sodom and Gomorrah?

9. Show from the entire passage we have studied how God is both just and merciful.

10. Using the examples of Abraham and Lot, list some ways in which you can show God that you take his judgment of sin seriously.

11. From your own experience, give an example of God's mercy.

Read Genesis 19:30-38 on you own. As you read, think about what factors may have contributed to this tragic story.

HOW DOES GOD FULFILL HIS PROMISES?

Genesis 20–21

1. Has God used difficult circumstances or long periods of waiting in your life to teach you? How?

Read Genesis 20.

♦ **2.** What were some of the reasons for Abraham and Sarah's deception?

3. On what grounds would you criticize their actions?

On what grounds did Abimelech, the unbeliever, criticize them?

4. When do you find it hardest to do the right thing?

5. What should Abraham have learned from his previous similar experience?

6. Are there any ways in which your present habits, or life-style, fail to reflect your actual experience with God?

Read Genesis 21.

7. What good things resulted from God's allowing Abraham and Sarah to wait until now for Isaac to be born?

8. How does seeing God fulfill long-range promises help you when you're feeling discouraged or purposeless?

9. What problems result from Abraham and Sarah's attempt to do God's job for him (verses 8-10)?

10. For what reasons did God preserve Ishmael?

11. To whom did God show his graciousness in these two chapters? In what ways?

12. In what ways has God intervened when you've made mistakes?

WHY IS IT WORTHWHILE TO KEEP ON TRUSTING GOD?

Genesis 22

1. What kinds of things are you afraid of?

Read Genesis 22.

   2. What did God command Abraham?

   3. Did God realize what he was asking of Abraham? How do you know (verse 2)?

♦ **4.** What was at stake for Abraham in obeying this command? (See also Genesis 21:12.)

5. What details in this account emphasize Abraham's wholehearted, unhesitating response?

6. Why do you think Abraham was able to obey God?

7. What test from God did Abraham pass (verse 12)?

8. In what ways did Abraham benefit from being tested?

♦ **9.** What does it mean to "fear God"?

10. Recalling your answer to question 1, how is fearing God different from those fears?

How does fearing God help you handle the things you are afraid of?

11. In what ways does God give emphasis to his promise to Abraham?

Can you think of any reasons why God would restate his promise to Abraham at this time?

12. In what different ways does God remind you of his promises to you?

HOW DOES MY LIFE SHOW CONFIDENCE IN GOD?

Genesis 23:1–25:11

1. How would you describe one of the main goals in your life?

Read Genesis 23.

2. From verses 4-6, describe Abraham's position in the community.

◆ **3.** How do the parts of this ancient legal transaction correspond to modern practices?

♦ **Read Genesis 24.**

   4. What was Abraham's main concern in getting a wife
   for Isaac?

♦ **5.** How do each of Abraham's commands to his servant
   (verses 1-9) reveal how much Abraham trusted God?

   6. Through what sign did the servant ask the Lord to show
   him the right girl? What information would he know
   about the girl's character if she fulfilled this sign?

   7. How is Rebekah introduced in verses 15-16?

   8. What more do we learn about her qualities that show
   her promise of being a good wife for Isaac?

9. In this chapter, what examples do you see of people recognizing the Lord's hand in events and trusting him?

10. What qualities do you have to fit you for the role the Lord has assigned to you?

Read Genesis 25:1-11.

11. What is the mood of these last statements about Abraham's life? In what ways was Abraham's life a complete and full one?

12. What kinds of things need to happen in your life in order for you to feel that it has been full and complete?

PART THREE

JACOB

Following Abraham's death, his son Ishmael settles near Egypt, while Isaac and Rebekah continue to live in Canaan. God's blessing is passed on to Isaac, and then to Jacob. As you follow Jacob's journeys from place to place, you will also track his spiritual pilgrimage. He had a long way to go as God prepared him to be *Israel,* heir of the promises made to Abraham.

At many points, Jacob seems an unlikely representative of God's chosen people. But God appears to him again and again, affirming his covenant and reminding Jacob of his place in the divine plan. As you watch him struggle with God, you will see Jacob change from a scheming deceiver to a God-governed man, and you will thank God for this example of his infinite grace.

WHAT DOES GOD LOOK FOR IN FAMILY RELATIONSHIPS?

Genesis 25:19–28:9

1. In what ways are you like your father or mother?

Read Genesis 25:19-34.

2. How might Rebekah have felt after the Lord described her unborn sons?

◆ **3.** What were the weaknesses of Esau and Jacob? What were their strengths?

♦ **Read Genesis 26.**

4. How did Isaac show he was Abraham's son:
—in the way he trusted God (see Genesis 12)?

—in his weakness?

—in his relationships with the world around him?

—in his material wealth?

Read Genesis 27:1–28:9.

5. What was Rebekah's plan? Why did she do this?

Did her plan work?

6. Compare the blessings given to Jacob and Esau. How was each blessing worthwhile?

7. What resulted from Jacob's fleeing to Paddan Aram? Why did Esau respond as he did?

8. How would you describe the root problem in this family? How did each family member contribute to the problem?

9. What do *you* do that causes tension at home?

10. What could you do to encourage peacefulness in your home?

HOW DOES GOD BRING US TO MATURITY?

Genesis 28:10–30:43

1. When in your life have you experienced the greatest spiritual growth?

Read Genesis 28:10–29:30.

2. How did God identify himself to Jacob and make his promise personal?

3. Remembering why Jacob was on the road, why was this an effective time for God to speak? Evaluate Jacob's response.

4. What events led to Jacob's agreeing to work for Laban for seven years?

5. How does the text indicate how much Jacob loved Rachel?

Read Genesis 29:31–30:43.

6. Why did Jacob agree to stay after he had "earned" his wives? What were the terms of his contract with Laban?

♦ **7.** Describe Jacob's home life (29:31–30:24). How would you characterize Leah and Rachel's relationship?

8. Suggest several one-word descriptions of Laban. Support your choice with specific details from the chapter.

9. Think back over Jacob's life. In what ways were Jacob and Laban alike?

10. In what ways was God maturing Jacob to be a spiritually fit spiritual successor to Abraham?

11. What means does God use to mature people today? How are you growing in your faith?

12. Pray together, thanking God for what he is doing in your lives, and asking him to continue to help you grow spiritually.

WHAT DOES GOD DESIRE IN RELATIONSHIPS?

Genesis 31

1. Describe a time when you resolved tension in a difficult relationship. How did it feel?

Read Genesis 31.

2. What factors led Jacob and his wives to agree that it was time to leave Laban's house?

3. Imagine you are Laban. What reasons do you have for being hurt and angry when you hear Jacob and his family have left?

4. What happened when Laban caught up with Jacob?

How do you think Laban's encounter with Jacob might have been different if God had not spoken to Laban?

♦ **5.** What are some possible reasons for Rachel's taking the household gods?

6. Was Jacob's righteous indignation justified (verses 36-42)?

7. How did the confrontation between Jacob and Laban end? (Follow events through the end of the chapter.) What were the terms of the covenant? Does this agreement shed any new light on Laban's character?

8. In what specific ways was each member of the family better off because he or she didn't have to live with the results of running away?

9. What happens in a relationship when you don't resolve tension?

10. Think of a relationship in your life that has been marred by deceit, selfishness, or defensiveness. Without explaining the history of the relationship, mention one thing you could do to make it possible to "eat together," as Jacob and Laban did.

HOW DO I KNOW GOD'S PLANS ARE GOOD?

Genesis 32–33

1. Think of a meeting or encounter that you dreaded. What was the outcome?

Read Genesis 32.

2. What reasons, up to this point, did Jacob have for knowing that God would support him in his encounter with Esau?

What additional reasons does he now have?

3. How did Jacob prepare to meet Esau? Because of his past actions, what might his fears have been?

4. How do past wrongs you've committed affect your attitudes toward other people?

5. How was his encounter the following night (verses 22-31) a sign that God had heard his prayer?

6. What might Jacob have learned about himself and about God during this crucial struggle?

Note: The name Israel *means "he struggles with God."*

Read Genesis 33.

7. How was Esau's reception different from what Jacob was expecting?

8. What had happened to Esau in the past twenty years? How do you know? (Examine Esau's actions through verse 16.)

♦ **9.** Why would Jacob want to get his family settled before visiting his brother?

10. Look at Jacob's original bargain with God in 28:18-22. To what degree had each party kept his part of the bargain?

11. How does seeing God's hand working in our lives for good affect our relationship with God? With other people? With ourselves?

12. How did Jacob say God had dealt with him (verse 11)? Can you say the same thing about God's dealing with you? Why?

HOW DO WE MEET GOD?

Genesis 34:1–36:8

1. If you were to go back to an actual place in your past that was important to you spiritually, where would it be? What made it significant?

Read Genesis 34.

2. If you had to vote for "good guys" in this story, who would you vote for?

♦ **3.** What examples do you see of people acting out of mixed motives?

4. How did Jacob's sons show disrespect for their father?

5. What was Jacob's concern after this incident? What else was at stake?

Read Genesis 35:1–36:8.

6. What are the major events in the lives of Jacob, Rachel, and Esau in this passage?

◆ **7.** What elements in this story show God's desire for Jacob to worship him?

8. What did Jacob do to prepare for his meeting with God at Bethel (35:2-6)?

Note: Bethel *means "house of God."*

9. How do you prepare to worship God?

10. Why is it sometimes helpful to go to a special place to meet God?

11. At what times does it help to meditate on God's promises and recount them to other people?

12. What Scripture has God used in speaking to you, and why is it particularly meaningful? (You are not limited to these chapters on Jacob's life.)

PART FOUR

JOSEPH

One of the youngest of Jacob's twelve sons, Joseph was dearly loved by his father and especially hated by his brothers. As he becomes a major player in God's plan, Joseph experiences more than enough hardships to destroy a person—yet he triumphs over them. As you follow him in his roles as son, brother, slave, and administrator, you will observe his moral and spiritual strength. It will be clear that "the LORD was with him" (Genesis 39:21).

Interwoven through Joseph's story is the continuation of Jacob's pilgrimage, to the point where he stands before Pharaoh, bestowing his blessing, conscious of his place as the representative of the Almighty. The story of Jacob and Joseph is really the story of how God works in history. With Jacob's family in Egypt, the stage is set for the great exodus to the Promised Land.

HOW DO I REACT TO PRESSURE?

Genesis 37

1. How did you get along with your brothers and sisters when you were growing up?

◆ **Read Genesis 37.**

2. What are the evidences in verses 1-4 of troubled family relationships?

3. Imagine the family at supper together. What are some things the brothers might *not* say to Joseph? What are some things they *might* say?

4. Think of someone you have been angry with recently. How did you show your displeasure?

5. Why did Joseph's dreams make his brothers hate him even more (verses 5-11)? Are there any indications here that they thought the dreams were more serious than just the imagination of a spoiled younger brother (verses 8, 11, 18-20)?

♦ **6.** What motives do you see at work in the different brothers' actions toward Joseph?

7. How did the brothers cover their tracks? What more does this tell us of their character?

8. How do you respond when someone seems to be threatening your position in a group?

9. How do you think Joseph felt as he sat in the cistern and perhaps heard some of the conversation?

10. What various possibilities could Joseph have imagined about his future? (Go through to the end of the chapter.)

11. Are you surprised when you experience situations that look and feel hopeless? How can you prepare for them?

12. What hopeless or pressured situation are you facing now? What encouragement does God's care and love offer you?

Read Genesis 38 on your own. We have skipped it in this study because it breaks the continuity of Joseph's story. The chapter is important as family history, for it settles the seniority of the tribe of Judah and allows us to see the messianic lineage of Jesus develop. Chapter 38 also contrasts Judah's immoral behavior with Joseph's faith and integrity.

HOW CAN I BE SURE OF GOD'S STEADFAST LOVE?

Genesis 39–40

1. Describe a time when you experienced or witnessed a great injustice. How did you respond?

Read Genesis 39–40.

2. What problems and tensions did Joseph face as he fulfilled his responsibilities in Potiphar's house?

◆ **3.** What kept Joseph from giving in to temptation with Potiphar's wife (39:8-12)? What sacrifice did he make to preserve his personal integrity?

4. In what situation are you both a servant and in authority? What temptations do you face in these situations, and how do you handle them?

5. What kind of injustices had Joseph faced in his life up to this point?

6. If you were an innocent Hebrew with an all-powerful God, how would you handle being sent to prison? How did Joseph seem to handle it?

7. In spite of his own problems, how did Joseph show concern for others?

8. Why was Joseph confident that he could interpret the dreams of the cupbearer and baker (40:8)?

9. What factors enabled Joseph to cope with disappointment? What do you admire most about him?

10. In what ways does God want you to be like Joseph?

11. How can you grow in these areas?

What kind of help can you expect from God?

12. Pray together, and ask the Lord to help you trust him in all circumstances.

WHAT ARE THE CHARACTERISTICS OF GOD'S MATURE PERSON?

Genesis 41

1. When did the responsibilities of adulthood first hit you?

Read Genesis 41.

2. How did both of Pharaoh's dreams emphasize the severity and certainty of the famine?

3. In what ways were Joseph's reactions to the dreams similar to those of Pharaoh and the rest of the court? In what ways did his reaction differ from theirs?

4. Why did Pharaoh believe Joseph? How did Pharaoh know his appointment of Joseph was justified?

◆ **5.** How did Pharaoh help Joseph do the job to which he appointed him (verses 41-44)?

6. What characteristics in Joseph allowed others to entrust him with responsibility?

7. What can you do now to be someone who can be given increasing responsibility?

8. How do his children's names reflect God's work in Joseph's life?

9. What evidence is there from this chapter that Joseph's life was satisfying?

10. What does God provide that makes your life whole and helps you mature? How will you recognize that wholeness?

WHAT IS NECESSARY FOR RECONCILIATION?

Genesis 42:1–45:15

1. Describe a time when you were separated from your family for a significant amount of time. What was it like to be reunited again?

Read Genesis 42:1-8.

♦ **2.** After these twenty years, what gaps or barriers would there be between Joseph and his brothers?

3. What has to happen on both sides before a reconciliation can be real?

*In order to understand what is involved in reconciliation,
read the following story of Joseph and his brothers in sec-
tions, using the questions to direct your thinking toward
the process of reconciliation.*

Read Genesis 42:9-24.

4. What pressures do the brothers feel in this section? In
what ways does it make them relive the past?

Read Genesis 42:25 – 43:14.

5. Why would finding money in their sacks dismay them?
What are some evidences that the brothers are beginning
to accept responsibility?

Read Genesis 43:15 – 45:3.

6. In what different ways do the brothers react to Joseph's
authority before and during the feast?

7. What finally convinced Joseph that his brothers were not the same as they were when they sold him into slavery?

8. Name the ways Joseph displayed generosity and a willingness to forgive his brothers. (Think of all the Scripture we've covered so far.)

9. What elements have we seen so far in the process of reconciliation?

Read Genesis 45:4-15.

10. How did Joseph convince his brothers that his forgiveness was genuine?

11. Think of someone who has hurt you. Without sharing the specific situation, what do you need to be and do in order to forgive that person?

HOW CAN I RECOGNIZE GOD'S PURPOSES IN MY LIFE?

Genesis 45:16–47:31

1. If you can, describe a time when, looking back, you've been able to see God's purpose or care in a particular situation.

Read Genesis 45:16–46:7.

2. In what ways was Pharaoh's attitude a real advantage to Joseph and his family?

3. What problems did the brothers have in convincing their father to come to Egypt?

---

4. Of what things did Jacob need to be assured before he left his home in Canaan? How did God provide for these needs?

Read Genesis 46:26–47:12.

♦ **5.** Why would Joseph want to keep his family from living right in the middle of the Egyptian community? How might you expect a foreign country to react to a tribe of Hebrews coming to live with them—especially considering the national crisis?

6. What are the evidences that God prepared the way for Joseph and his family in Egypt?

Read Genesis 47:13-31.

7. What were the progressive effects of the famine on the Egyptian people? How did Joseph fulfill his responsibilities to Pharaoh? To the Egyptian people?

8. In what ways had Jacob's life been hard?

♦ **9.** Review God's promise to Jacob in Genesis 28:13-15. What were God's purposes for the descendants of Jacob that guaranteed his protection for their survival and growth?

10. In what ways does today's study encourage you to trust God's purposes and promises?

HOW HAS GOD BLESSED ME?

Genesis 48–49

1. Is there an older person in your life whom you especially respect? How does his or her life bless you?

Read Genesis 48.

    2. How did Jacob honor Joseph and his family?

    3. What was there about his father's blessing that displeased Joseph (verses 17-20)? How might Jacob's response reassure Joseph?

Read Genesis 49.

4. According to each blessing, what did Jacob know about the character of his sons?

5. Mention several details in the blessings that go beyond Jacob's personal knowledge of his sons.

♦ **6.** How was each son's future shaped by his past actions?

♦ **7.** Discover all the references that Jacob made to God in these two chapters. What experiences with God do each of these references reflect? (Try to think of specifics from Jacob's life.)

8. From these references, what had Jacob learned about God's character during his lifetime?

9. What have you experienced of God's character? Give him a name or title that expresses your experience with him. (ex., "the God who comes through in a pinch")

10. In what ways has God blessed you? How has he shown you who he is?

11. Pray short sentence prayers, thanking God for what he has shown you.

WHAT HAVE I LEARNED ABOUT GOD?

Genesis 49:29–50:26

1. If you knew you were going to die soon, what instructions would you give to your family?

Read Genesis 49:29–50:26.

2. How did Jacob prepare to die? (Take into account Genesis 48–49.) What was the prevailing mood that he set for his departure from this life?

3. How did other people react to his death? (Look at all the reactions.)

4. How were the brothers still affected by past sins (50:15-17)?

◆ **5.** Why could Joseph forgive them so completely?

6. What other effects of sin have you noticed in your study of Jacob and Joseph? (Be specific.)

7. How did God deal with and overcome sin in these lives?

8. What attributes of God did Joseph emphasize to his brothers (50:15-26)?

Closing Thoughts

9. What attributes of God stand out in your mind from your study of Genesis?

10. What have you learned about your spiritual roots in this book of "beginnings"? What have you learned about your faith?

11. Close in prayer, praising God for what he has revealed of himself to you in these studies.

LEADER'S NOTES

Study 1/What Does It Mean to Live in God's World?

Note on Genesis 1. There are many views held as to the historicity and literalness of this account of creation. For the purposes of this study, we are by-passing the creationism versus evolution debate. The biblical account establishes that God is the initiator and Creator, and that is all we wish to assert.

Question 6. The term *image* used here states "intensively the fact that man uniquely reflects God. . . . by creation man bears an image actually corresponding to the divine original" (Carl F. H. Henry, *The Evangelical Dictionary of Theology,* p. 546. Grand Rapids, Mich.: Baker Book House, 1984). We reflect God's glory, and aspects of our humanity—reason, creativity, ability to love, eternal souls—are ways we bear God's image. This belief provides a foundation for the dignity of life and our self-worth.

Study 2/How Does God Meet Our Needs?

Question 5. There are many speculations as to the meaning of the tree of the knowledge of good and evil. But for the purposes of this study, it is sufficient to observe that it was forbidden, and thus gave Adam and Eve an opportunity to obey God or choose not to obey.

Question 9. "The naming of the animals, a scene which portrays man as monarch of all he surveys, poignantly reveals him as a social being, made for fellowship, not power: he will not live until he loves, giving himself away (Genesis 2:24) to another on his own level. So the woman is presented wholly as his partner and counterpart; nothing is yet said of her as childbearer. She is valued for herself alone" (Derek Kidner, *Genesis,* The Tyndale Old Testament Commentary Series, D.J. Wiseman, gen. ed., p. 65. Chicago: InterVarsity Press, 1967).

▓ Study 3/Why Is Disobeying God So Serious?

Question 2. In Genesis 3, the author expresses important things about God's view of disobedience and its consequences. Many people may feel at this point that they can understand the truth of the principles that are taught in this chapter without fully accepting the smaller components of the story as actual, detailed history. Christ and Paul accepted the historicity of Adam and Eve, as have Christians of all traditions. See Matthew 19:4-5; Romans 5:12-15.

▓ Study 4/What Is My Response to Sin?

Note on Genesis 4. Have the group concentrate particularly on Cain as they read.

Question 3. Some people believe Cain's offering was not accepted because it was not a blood sacrifice and, as the Bible later teaches, blood must be shed for the forgiveness of sins (Hebrews 9:22). However, seeking pardon for sin is not the only reason to bring an offering to God. Other times God asks for first-fruit offerings, cereal offerings, and thank offerings, as in Leviticus 23:9-14 and Deuteronomy 26:1-11. A major thrust of biblical teaching about sacrifice to God is that the *attitude* with which the offering is given is more important than the content of the offering (see 1 Samuel 15:22; Isaiah 1:11-20).

Question 6. Note that murdering Abel was only one element in the sequence of Cain's sin.

■ Study 5/What Is It Like to Walk with God in a Sinful World?

Question 2. "Does this mean that God regretted creating humanity? Was he admitting he made a mistake? No, God does not change his mind (1 Samuel 15:29). Instead, he was expressing sorrow for what the people had done to themselves, as a parent might express sorrow over a rebellious child. God was sorry that the people chose sin and death instead of a relationship with him" *(Life Application Bible,* p. 18. Wheaton, Ill.: Tyndale House Publishers, 1988).

Question 3. "To say that Noah was *righteous* and *blameless* does not mean that he never sinned (the Bible records one of his sins in Genesis 9:20-28). Rather it means that he wholeheartedly loved and obeyed God. For a lifetime he walked step by step in faith as a living example to his generation" *(Life Application Bible,* p. 18).

■ Study 6/How Does My Walk with God Affect Others?

Question 9. It is all right to recognize that God really does use you. Encourage people to be specific about how he is doing this.

Question 11. The Bible doesn't portray whitewashed saints, but real people. Encourage group members to reflect both on the realistic narrative of the Scriptures and also the need to continue a close walk with God, especially after significant "successes" in our lives.

■ Study 7/What Is the Response of Faith?

Note on Genesis 12:10-20. A similar situation comes up again in Genesis 20. We'll deal with it in more detail then.

■ Study 8/What Is Involved in Believing God?

Question 5. A typical means of publicly attesting to a two-party agreement in Abram's day was for the parties involved to pass between the severed halves of animals, saying through their actions something like this: "May I be as dead as these bodies if I break our contract." Today we sign a legal form in the presence of a notary public.

Question 7. Sarah's suggestion that Abram take Hagar was according to the customs of the day. Sometimes a marriage contract even required a barren wife to buy a slave woman for her husband. The legality of this action, however, did not justify their lack of faith and patience.

■ Study 9/What Does It Mean to Be in a Covenant Relationship with God?

Note on Genesis 17. As you read, have the group look for the specific information and commands God gives Abram to assure him that God wants a continuing relationship with him.

Question 3. Note that God changed their names here. *Abram* means "exalted father," and *Abraham* means "father of many." *Sarai* and *Sarah* are forms of the same word meaning "princess," but this naming brought Sarah into the covenantal promise in her own right.

Question 8. Look up *covenant* in a dictionary and read the definition to your group as you discuss this question.

■ Study 11/How Does God Fulfill His Promises?

Question 2. This deception occurs some twenty-four years after the similar incident in Egypt (Genesis 12:10-20). Group members may note that in both cases, fear and lack of trust are at the root of Abraham's problems.

■ Study 12/Why Is It Worthwhile to Keep On Trusting God?

Question 4. God's covenant with Abraham rested on his promised son, Isaac.

Question 9. To fear God means we have a reverential awe of him that makes us want to obey him and keep from displeasing him.

■ Study 13/How Does My Life Show Confidence in God?

Question 3. Abraham was bargaining politely with Ephron, as was the custom. If Abraham had taken the land without paying, it would have insulted Ephron.

Note on Genesis 24. Because chapter 24 is so long, it might be helpful to divide up the reading between two people (with the break coming at verse 33).

Question 5. The person who takes an oath is invoking a curse upon himself if he breaks his word. Some scholars suggest that because God's name was called on, God was committed to take action against the oathbreaker. Placing a hand under the thigh was a particularly solemn form of oath that symbolically called on the man's descendants to stand witness, a swearing by his posterity.

■ Study 14/What Does God Look for in Family Relationships?

Question 3. The birthright was a status symbol, given to the first-born. It meant the headship of the family and, in some cases later, a double share of the estate.

Note on Genesis 26. This is a long study and you may want to use the questions on Genesis 26 for your own study, and then summarize the action and the main point for the group.

Study 15/How Does God Bring Us to Maturity?

Question 7. "In his family relations Jacob continued to sow bitter seed. His coolness to his unwanted wife was understandable, but Genesis 29:31ff. shows what God as well as Leah thought of it, and there are few things more pathetic than the naming of her first three sons. . . . On the human plane the history demonstrates the craving of human beings for love and recognition, and the price of thwarting it; on the divine level it shows once again the grace of God choosing difficult and unpromising material" *(Genesis,* p. 161.)

Study 16/What Does God Desire in Relationships?

Question 5. Rachel may have taken the idols for religious reasons, or to strengthen her claim to an inheritance she thought was her due (see Genesis 31:14).

Study 17/How Do I Know God's Plans Are Good?

Question 9. There are two critical views of Jacob's actions at this point. One school of thought suggests he is being devious and scheming again, promising to come to his brother's house when obviously he is not intending to. The other view suggests that the words exchanged between the brothers are in part courtesy, indicating amicable relationships, but also recognizing that although their families and herds are too big to occupy the same territory (see Genesis 36:6-8), they will enjoy each other's hospitality at mutually convenient times.

Study 18/How Do We Meet God?

Question 3. The differing reactions to Dinah's defilement by Jacob and his sons (Genesis 34:30-31) exemplify two typical but futile reactions to evil: fear and revenge.

Question 7. Jacob's concern in Genesis 34 was for his personal safety. He didn't seem to be concerned for God's honor and reputation. Yet God called Jacob and his family back to himself and to a renewed commitment at his altar.

Study 19/How Do I React to Pressure?

Note on Genesis 37. As you read, notice whose emotions are recorded, and what they are.

Question 6. Though it seems Reuben felt some remorse and had feelings for Joseph (Genesis 37:21-22, 29-30), it was also true that as the eldest he would have been held mainly responsible for any bloodshed.

Study 20/How Can I Be Sure of God's Steadfast Love?

Question 3. One commentary notes that Joseph's reasons for refusal—his trusted freedom in the household, and his rapid rise to position—might have been the very reasons other stewards *would* have yielded to Potiphar's wife. In addition, Joseph recognized the proposal for what it was: sin against God.

Study 21/What Are the Characteristics of God's Mature Person?

Question 5. Joseph's position over the whole land is generally held to be that of a vizier. "The signet ring carried the king's authority. . .

the fine linen was court dress. A gold chain was a customary mark of royal appreciation. . . . The *second chariot* clearly proclaims him the next after Pharaoh" *(Genesis,* pp. 196–97).

■ Study 22/What Is Necessary for Reconciliation?

Question 2. Joseph is by this time close to forty years old. He was seventeen when he was sold into slavery (Genesis 37:2), thirty when he entered Pharaoh's service (41:46), and the seven years of plenty have passed.

■ Study 23/How Can I Recognize God's Purposes in My Life?

Question 5. Goshen was an unsettled land east of the Nile Delta, loosely attached to Egypt.

Question 9. The New Testament tells us that if we belong to Christ then we are Abraham's descendants, as Jacob was, and so we too are heirs according to God's promise (Galatians 3:14, 29).

■ Study 24/How Has God Blessed Me?

Question 6. See Genesis 35:22 for reference to Reuben's past; Genesis 34 for Simeon and Levi; Genesis 37:8ff. for Joseph. The preeminence of the tribes of Judah and Joseph is shown in their prominent blessings.

Question 7. Let the group work through the chapters to find these references. They include Genesis 48:3-4; 48:11; 48:15-16; 48:20-21; 49:18; 49:24-25.

▇ Study 25/What Have I Learned About God?

Question 5. Joseph was able to let go of resentments and trust God for the results. He leaves all "the righting of one's wrongs to God. . . sees [God's] providence in man's malice, . . . and repays evil not only with forgiveness but also with practical affection" *(Genesis,* p. 224).

WHAT SHOULD WE STUDY NEXT?

To help your group answer that question, we've listed the
Fisherman Guides by category so you can choose your next study.

TOPICAL STUDIES

Angels, Wright

Becoming Women of Purpose,
  Barton

Building Your House on the Lord,
  Brestin

Discipleship, Reapsome

Doing Justice, Showing Mercy,
  Wright

Encouraging Others, Johnson

Examining the Claims of Jesus,
  Brestin

Friendship, Brestin

The Fruit of the Spirit, Briscoe

Great Doctrines of the Bible,
  Board

Great Passages of the Bible,
  Plueddemann

Great Prayers of the Bible,
  Plueddemann

**Growing Through Life's
  Challenges,** Reapsome

Guidance & God's Will, Stark

Heart Renewal, Goring

Higher Ground, Brestin

Lifestyle Priorities, White

Marriage, Stevens

Miracles, Castleman

Moneywise, Larsen

One Body, One Spirit, Larsen

The Parables of Jesus, Hunt

Prayer, Jones

The Prophets, Wright

Proverbs & Parables, Brestin

Satisfying Work, Stevens &
  Schoberg

Senior Saints, Reapsome

Sermon on the Mount, Hunt

Spiritual Warfare, Moreau

The Ten Commandments,
  Briscoe

Who Is God? Seemuth

Who Is the Holy Spirit?
  Knuckles & Van Reken

Who Is Jesus? Van Reken

Witnesses to All the World,
  Plueddemann

Worship, Sibley

BIBLE BOOK STUDIES

Genesis, Fromer & Keyes

Job, Klug

Psalms, Klug

Proverbs: Wisdom That Works, Wright

Ecclesiastes, Brestin

Jonah, Habakkuk, & Malachi, Fromer & Keyes

Matthew, Sibley

Mark, Christensen

Luke, Keyes

John: Living Word, Kuniholm

Acts 1-12, Christensen

Paul (Acts 13-28), Christensen

Romans: The Christian Story, Reapsome

1 Corinthians, Hummel

Strengthened to Serve (2 Corinthians), Plueddemann

Galatians, Titus & Philemon, Kuniholm

Ephesians, Baylis

Philippians, Klug

Colossians, Shaw

Letters to the Thessalonians, Fromer & Keyes

Letters to Timothy, Fromer & Keyes

Hebrews, Hunt

James, Christensen

1 & 2 Peter, Jude, Brestin

How Should a Christian Live? (1, 2 & 3 John), Brestin

Revelation, Hunt

BIBLE CHARACTER STUDIES

David: Man after God's Own Heart, Castleman

Elijah, Castleman

Great People of the Bible, Plueddemann

King David: Trusting God for a Lifetime, Castleman

Men Like Us, Heidebrecht & Scheuermann

Paul (Acts 13-28), Christensen

Peter, Castleman

Ruth & Daniel, Stokes

Women Like Us, Barton

Women Who Achieved for God, Christensen

Women Who Believed God, Christensen